the heart, the border

Books by Ken Smith

The Pity (Jonathan Cape, 1967)
Work, distances/poems (Swallow Press, Chicago, 1972)
Tristan Crazy (Bloodaxe Books, 1978)
Fox Running (Bloodaxe Books, 1981)
Burned Books (Bloodaxe Books, 1981)
Abel Baker Charlie Delta Epic Sonnets (Bloodaxe Books, 1982)
The Poet Reclining: Selected Poems (Bloodaxe Books, 1982)
Terra (Bloodaxe Books, 1986)
A Book of Chinese Whispers (Bloodaxe Books, 1987)
Wormwood (Bloodaxe Books, 1987)
Inside Time (Harrap, 1989; Mandarin 1990)
The heart, the border (Bloodaxe Books, 1990)
Berlin: Coming in from the Cold (Hamish Hamilton, 1990;
Penguin, 1991)

KEN SMITH

the heart,
the border

BLOODAXE BOOKS

ISBN: 1 85224 139 X

First published 1990 by
Bloodaxe Books Ltd,
P.O. Box 1SN,
Newcastle upon Tyne NE99 1SN.

Bloodaxe Books Ltd acknowledges
the financial assistance of Northern Arts.

Typesetting by Bryan Williamson, Darwen, Lancashire.

Printed in Great Britain by
Bell & Bain Limited, Glasgow, Scotland.

ENG
R 53472 A

I.M. Millicent Emma Smith, 1911-1990
&
I.M. Asa Benveniste, 1925-1990
  'a city man
  who can no longer tell the difference
  between traffic and silence'

Acknowledgements

Acknowledgements are due to the editors of the following publications in which some of these poems first appeared: *Bête Noire, Critical Quarterly, Margin, Numbers, Pivot, PN Review, Poetry Review, Poetry Wales, Sunk Island Review* and *Words*. Acknowledgements are also due to the following anthologies in which some poems have also appeared: *Against the grain* (Nelson); *Assemblage* (University of Essex); *High on the Walls: a Morden Tower anthology* (Morden Tower/Bloodaxe Books, 1990); *The New British Poetry* (Paladin, 1988); *The Poetry Book Society Anthology 1988/89* and *1990/91* (PBS/Hutchinson, 1989 & 1990).

The author acknowledges assistance from the Arts Council of Great Britain.

Contents

In the Evangelical Cemetery, San Michele, Venice:

Sacred to the memory of
Archibald Campbell
Master of the SY Minerva
Who died on board
March 17 1891
Aged 56

*

*The heart knoweth its
own bitterness, and the
stranger intermeddleth
not therewith.*

Dorothea Extempore

I am a citizen of an incurious land. While everything changes, this does not change: we accept the customs of our ancestors. We are born, we are named. From infancy to adolescence it is explained to us, patiently, over and over, what are the three things we must do, and this is our whole education and all our lives thereafter: first we must plant a tree, and second we must begin to make a rope. Thus each of us has a rope, each of us has a tree. For each, the rope's first thread is the umbilical that spun us from our mothers, and as we grow we must gather and plant the seeds to grow the hemp to make the fibre from which to spin the braids of the rope, weaving into it the stray hair of all those we love and some we do not love and some – it turned out – who never loved us. Making such a rope takes many years. Meanwhile we must tend the tree: the roots, the trunk, the bark, the branches, twigs, the leaves, the fruit and the seeds, and whatever birds and animals and insects live among them, the dawn singers and the evening moths, the cicadas in their long cycles down among the roots for 17 years, and whatever plants grow there in the shade. Later, when we and the trees are grown tall enough and the rope grown long enough, we learn what is the third thing we must do: we must take one and hang ourselves on the other. And somehow sooner or later, one way or another, each of us ends up doing just that.

Writing in prison

Years ago I was a gardener.
I grew the flowers of my childhood,
lavender and wayside lilies
and my first love the cornflower.

The wind on the summer wheat.
The blue glaze in the vanished woods.
In the space of my yard I glimpsed again
all the lost places of my life.

I was remaking them. Here in a space
smaller still I make them again.

Greetings from the Winter Palace

Once he'd won a medal, he had a letter
proved it. He'd had a wife and a wedding.
He came and went, talking with his hands,
with all his names and all of them lies, alibis.

Call him Bob, call him Bounce, call him Dodge,
he's up again and down again. He says
beneath his breath *if you want to know the time
ask a policeman.* He has a problem and a needle

and he steals to keep it sharp. He writes
from his next station of the cross
*I'm in the Ville not treading on the star.
I dream of snow, of Acapulco, any fix.*

And then he's fading to a scrawl, the number
that he goes by, gesture of his mouth,
his hands folding on his hands. Then he's gone,
another junkie, another star no light comes back from.

Jack's postcards

Just a line of posts along the baymouth,
and the tide out. And I'm supposed to know
what they mean, this ship, this flag,
both departing on the horizon, this message.

I'm being tested. I'm under observation,
interpreting these picture postcards
sent by the nuns from Inveraray: *wish you
were here. But we pray for you.*

Pictures of cool green woods,
a thirst forever slaked beside the river,
a minaret, a market and a leaning tower,
and in the distance more the same –

the sunset over palms and best regards
from Disney World. You should know
the censor's on my shoulder always,
like the poor, like my angel, striking

what I cannot say in any case: does love
still hold each others' hands, does the heart burn,
or is the universe a glossy magazine
and all the polished girls bone china bright?

The pornographer

Three things the shrink said: he feared everyone,
he invented himself in everyone he met,
he feared sex. He'd pointed a camera at it
and ended up in jail, so much hot dry flesh
on the cold burned out eye of the lens.
For himself he loved no one, no one loved him.

They close their eyes, these lovers he's hired,
as if they were alone. They can act
no better than the rest of us, the way
they do it no one ever gets pregnant.
Watching, you wonder what the fees are,
who thought of Mozart by the Rome Symphony,
what they're on, what they say later
over coffee, cigarettes, Courvoisier
washing out the sweet spermy taste.

So this is how it is: flesh hungering for flesh,
fingers and tongues and all the cries,
so much juicy footage and white noise,
the soundtrack whimpering as if all life
wanted to be one and come again again,
smearing itself in itself. Meanwhile,
back at the big house the master with the maid,
the manservant with mother and daughter,
and the plot minimal. Like so many lives.
Sad thing for him this is the real thing.

Figures in three landscapes

One: *Brady at Saddleworth Moor*

Out, this is air, abrupt and everywhere,
the light and sky all one blaze of it.
Count them: eleven clear hours of wind
over the world's tops into my face –

this old bleached-out moon always adrift
through the bad dreams of the neighbourhood.
In my ten thousand days I count this day:
the moor, all its space and vastness

I hear them say I say. I find nothing
in all four corners of the wind
where stones haven't changed, tumps, gullies
one blue blur of heather and upland grass

where one grave looks much like another.
Think how many years the rain fell I felt
my heart in my chest a fist of sour dust
forming in the acids of my discontent.

But it knows one thought: nothing's forgot
though my vision's bad, my sanity debatable.
I can forget, I can remember, I can be mad,
I will never be as free again, ever.

Nor will anyone be free of me. Count on it.

Two: *Hungerford nights*

Before you get through this, before
the next page, before the next breath
you catch is the last breath:
the assassin's device has found you.

His knife of a heart has emptied your own.
Thereafter down the rest of the page: blood,
the book unreadable, plotless,
the tale of a man with a Kalashnikov.

How he soothes and greases it, nights
in the garden shed, a boy with a stick
in the bathroom mirror of his mind.
What he read, wore, saw on the video.

The symbols slip into their metal shoes,
oils groove the mechanism into one
precision milled moment, rapid fire
along the High St and you're dead.

And you're dead. And you're dead.
Himself he had difficulty with.
It ends with 16 red roses on his coffin,
one for each victim, like any cowboy.

His ashes scattered in an unknown place.

Three: *Murder at White House Farm*

So who am I now, falling nowhere
on my black wing in the black wind
calling my cry: *Innocent Innocent,*
may where was a murderer now grow a rose?

Can you find me, framed in a photograph
in the surf's eye on the world's other side,
riding the incoming water? I'm locked up now
in the grey tide of my heart's only season.

Singing my orphan song *Pity me Pity me,*
survivor of all I slaughtered, my years
closing before, the steel gates behind
I imagine a rose. I think of a kiss.

I consider the indifference of objects:
the knife killed a man carves bread
in his kitchen, the hammer
that clubbed him goes on sinking nails.

Here the clever ones dance and the smart ones
steal their money. We all go to the wall
known as *Anyone else,* and the stars
wander on in their merciless courses.

And no one calls out the seeds, we're all
God's wayward apprentices, miracles once,
thereafter mundanely repeated,
a lie telling a lie till one size fits all.

And all the words beyond this say farewell.

Against the grain

Someone must count them, the bodies that come up
one by one out of the fire, up from
the gloomy cradle of the North Sea
that has weighted and washed them, months.

Someone must number them, name each one
by the fingerprints, the rings, by the teeth,
someone must stare at the remnants of the dead
from Zeebrugge, Kings Cross, Piper Alpha:

more oil there than under all Arabia,
I recall long ago, *that we bought and paid for.*
We're dying of neglect. My country
is a free enterprise disaster zone.

And now someone must count them all: *one, one.*
Someone must zip them into a bag
and bury them, tally the ongoing total,
put up a stone. It goes against the grain.

Three Docklands fragments

1. *The Enterprise Zone*

On my birthday the snow wind
bringing feathery rain, a fine dust
falling on the edge of crystal.

I take the grey road along the river
where pass lives sadder than yours, mine,
slow death in the tower blocks.

These are the Silvertown Blues,
Fight the Rich ghosting out
in concrete, by the flyover.

No one ever gets straight here.
The ego's tale of itself is miserable,
nothing much happens but murder.

Yet that these wastes be repeopled
and the rich inherit, everyone's
moving downriver. This is *the zone*,

carved from the sour and floury air
of London's residuary body,
filling with cranes and dust

and the racket of money being made,
and there's nothing to say but to say
to myself *Thou bone, brother bone. You old bone.*

* *

2. *Of things to come*

Down the Bendy Road to Cyprus and Custom House
where the new cities rise from the drawing-boards
and the ghosts-to-be of George in his Capri,
JoJo in her birthday suit drinking white wine with soda
fly in from Paris for the weekend. Later
they'll gather with friends by the marina.
Later they'll appreciate the view of the river.
Later they'll jive to the mean mad dance of money
between the tower blocks over the runway
amongst the yachts already moored in the development.

* *

3. *Yuppy love*

What he calls her: my little pocket calculator
my fully portable my VDU my organiser my mouse
oh my filofax my cellnet my daisywheel.

What he dreams driving home at the wheel
on the brimming motorway: her electronics
the green screen of her underwear her digital display.

Oh my spreadsheet he groans in the night:
my modem my cursor lusting after her floppies
wanting her printout her linkup her entire database.

The New Management
(after Sean O'Brien, in his manner)

It's best they look tough in blue suits,
like police. They are anyway,
ordering the lights up, the heat down,
and you redundant. *We're letting you go,*

they say, *You're not in our cost centre.*
And you're not. You're out on the city's
skinny peripheries in the landscape
of windy bungalows. You don't live here

and of course it is raining. Entropy
was against you from the start and now
when you can't play the flute there's
only departure's uncountable sadness.

And they're watching. In other times
they marched in with banners and speeches,
read the new rules in their own rough tongue,
shot hostages, put up the salt tax.

Now they wear suits and the leader says
stand up, sit down and everyone dances.
They move to the music of money and leave
without introductions. Fact is

they're the missing witnesses to an accident
standing in the shade of the portico
to one side at the victim's funeral
in the Italian gardens, in dark glasses,

where one sniffs the roses, one shrugs,
another fondles a cigar he will smoke
over coffee, checking the till rolls,
later, the printout, the bottom line.

Which is you, wandering the empty quarter,
where you meet no one, you find nothing,
you return with no answers, only grit
in your teeth and a long thirst to slake.

Running on empty

What's it like? they ask.
Lots of space debris I reply: this music
has been written by psychologists.
'My name is Vera Lute, from Truth or Consequences.'

Some wander all their days
and never find the river.
So many lives are wasted and no one knows why.
That sounds to me like a crime.

Tell the BBC in confidence,
tell the golfing correspondent from *Angling Times*:
there were days when my heart was sore
and it always seemed to be raining.

Now there's too much to be angry about,
and no one left to forgive.
I'm the atheist at the bishop's conference.
I'm the fly in the ointment on the wall.

On and on down the dirty decades.
Nothing as described in the brochure,
as promised on the party platform
and nothing but bullshit to listen to.

My country is falling off the back of a lorry
but I bear you no malice, Alice.
What I'm in is chagrin. It's late,
I'm out on the road, running on empty.

And I'm calling you in.
I'm calling you in.

Imaginary confrontations

What a strange world Mother says,
stepping back into the room. We're still
talking about our sons – tall, handsome,
saying *just leave me be now Mother.*

That drink looks like a hedgehog
the cowboy says. Turning to me:
*is this your crow? You're as much use
as one trouser* I reply, *as half a pair of gloves.*

With that he puts The Inferno into his pocket
and gallops off across the map of Colorado,
I'm only here as an observer he announces.
I'm only part of the wiring in the wind.

This phone's bugged I say into the phone,
and this dream's rigged, to the people
living in the fibreoptic I've never met
who overhear us. Who knows who they talk to?

These days we talk funny, on the TV
discussing racket abuse in Latin America.
Suddenly I remember you in the bikini area,
and forget you again, wiping your tape into silence.

After the hurricane: how are things
in your wreck of the woods? Does the censor
know about you or were you educated locally?
Answers on a postcard. Wake me if I'm dreaming.

Intercepted letters: Harry inside

These words with difficulty, friend.
It's been a while. So little happens
through the slow harvests of time,
the abrupt inflexible silence at my door
there's no getting round. I make lists.
I add up columns of imaginary numbers.
I ponder the inscrutability of dice,
cards, horses, men. Maybe in the night
one thought thinks itself in my brain's
slow stunned contemplation of itself:
such a busy machine. It begins one end
of the room, it sweeps inch by inch
to the door then back again, it sifts
the junk, it inspects each matchstick,
finger paring, print, drop of blood,
pollen grain, every other dead roach.
It considers for, against, if, but,
maybe, and all I might have said, done.
It remembers what love was, the wind,
the banners of the seagrass, the old wheat
that was childhood, flesh falling
into flesh and the wars over, a moment.
It leaves nothing out and spares none of me,
the keys, locks, all the bricks, pipes,
bars, years, papers in the wind,
and all there never is to sing about,
to say nothing of the weather. What I do now
I keep my nose clean, a clean shirt
on the heating pipe and every day I work
mopping the wounds that go on being wounds
as the war goes on, day by day, so long now
we don't say *the war* any more.

Intercepted letters: Harry on the road

With one mighty bound I'm free, on the road
south and north, back from the border,
– skint again. I should be glad and am
yet each day I grow heavy, day by day
sinking closer to the earth's core.
Evenings the lights come on in the bars
where I'm no longer in residence
among the sour faces of the whisky drinkers,
men married to their fists, always hungry,
staring after the heels of women,
living in the ventilation system,
in the tape's hiss in the stereo.
That's how it is at the border:
ours an insanity we barely control,
a life all one fit of bad temper.
I saw fiend grab tot says the Sun.
I shall consider the ambivalence of a hat.
Oh I know, I'm all over this story,
I'm in and out the mask of myself.
All these words have been twice lost,
once in prison and once at the border.
They came home like me hungry in the rain.
There's where I met her: the drowned bride
in the bleak water, up from the country
from the deep freeze for the weekend's
brief encounter with imaginary friends.
How she moves I think she's the air
dressed in itself, she's shaped
like good bread, like geography
I'm lost in with other men like me.

Back from Leah's country

It's true I was in love: with the roads,
with the dry river beds and the canyons,
Joshua trees, mountains, sky, woods, snowline.
And you. We ran away together. Years ago.

It's true long after I'd look at your name
in secret, its winged calligraphy of wind,
smoke riding the air I dissolved in,
vanishing into the dark signature of your hair.

It's true I fucked you with my blood.
It's true later your name was a thought
that ran out. With you I was like you
without plan, without blueprint.

Like the cactus the repetition
of segments of itself, over and over.
I hate maps you said, and went off
into the desert expecting me to follow.

You would have taken me to Spider Mother's House
and filled me with your version of yourself.
You would have kept me in a room below the earth
and wrapped me in your silk till I was clean,

divided in departments of myself. It's true,
I was five parts hot air and no water
in the empty space between the slices of bread.
It was your darkness I was in love with.

Then when I came back I was mad, dumb,
lovesick, still drowning in the dry waterless air
of Leah's country. Now I'm myself
right side up there's even less to say about it.

We are what the rain sees, never
where we are but somewhere yesterday,
some other place we're on the way to,
anticipation turning into memory.

These events are put together backwards
from hints, shreds of evidence and hearsay,
restricted information, bias measured out
into the tight little shoes of language.

And it's too late to learn anything from them.
So there's an end to the affair.
Don't write. It's true this silence lasts
until we die. Let's not be friends.

The spectator's terrace, Gatwick

Maybe I came to consider distance,
departures, the hole in the sky
where plane after plane vanishes
into its promise of exotic arrivals.

On the ground the rain hisses,
the air sings with spent fuel,
travellers, strangers, saying *honey
it's best we both get insurance.*

Think of the miles of wiring,
the valves, pumps, connections,
blips on the radar, bolts
that shake loose, metal fatigue.

Up here on the spectator's terrace,
smug, aloof, not going anyplace,
I hang out with the cognoscenti
on a ten visit ticket for £2.50.

We inhabit the buffet,
bright city of darkened glass behind wind,
dreaming there's somewhere
to get to, anywhere else.

Here's where the blood clot strikes
and the end of all memory.
Here's where we all go out
in that grey sky the breeze is.

Then the heart

In the spring, working up and down
the enterprise zone, over the mountains
and over the mountains from one sea
to the other: sudden panic, in the chest's
left pocket a sharpness persisting into pain,
fear of more of it: of death's knife
and a surgeon's chainsaw to the breast,
and beyond the old fear it always was –
some moment I will die, and the universe
go on making light of itself.

Such an arrogance night after night
keeps me awake so I hang black hours
on my heart's thump and blood beat
at the sour lip of oblivion, in fear
that asleep I'll not wake to the last star,
the lost dream, the first birds of morning,
another day to write Tuesday's sonata,
Wednesday's epitaph, Saturday's lists
and my cherished Ode to a Month of Sundays.

*

* *

This pain: a crowbar to the chest. Small men
in black suits at the meeting of my ribcage
are forcing a door, muttering in a language
without a word for *No*. Now I can say
how Tom Thumb felt in the giant's fist
and what the cut worm won't forgive,
what the vampire howls with the stake
to the far side of his screaming. This pain
begins at the horizon, it begins
promising only more of itself, then
down the distance's swift oncoming
takes on the sudden likeness of wolves
in a slick dark river of fur pouring east
through the breastbone, left at the rib,
bunched down the shoulder, the arm, elbow,
wrist, knucklebones and out down the fingers
gnarled all the way, and beyond
more wolves coming.
                              Then it stops
like a toothache lugged all weekend
at last to the dentist, folds to a bat
hanging upside down in the ribs' raft,
a far off murmur of wolves, a snarling.

* *

* * *

I have no beginning. I arrived
in a white room of frightened men
sweating it out in white sheets. Here
in my skull I've this voice: the prompt,
pilot and navigator, backseat driver
yelling what to do. And my father
the northern puritan nagging *Work.*
Do something useful, son. It began
being his voice but now it is mine,
the disease of the pale Europeans
with their spades and measuring rods.
It killed him. It will kill me.

Insomniac, all my life a rehearsal,
my heart counting time at its post
not to miss the very last moment –
the trumpets, the strutting horses,
the drums and the brass band's last
Abide with me falling all at once
from the world without one more word,
thereafter part of the dust on the landings,
the full stop any time now where
to cease must at last cease itself:

    hush, now.

Why not here as at the beginning, circled
by these good women, among these pillows
and these clean white sheets, – so much care,
so much love in the scrubbed soft fingers
of the nurses, all of them so many colours
that are all of them blue? Why not here
among these sweet blue lilies?

* * *

* * * *

I have no beginning. Each day
is a beginning, an ending, a victory.
Each day a defeat. When I sleep
it is far back in the cave of myself
and I bring nothing back but the dream
of the hollow tree of my own curled self.
Some days I hold one thought, the blackbird
on the chimney singing we say
his heart out across the rooves
and washing lines of London's east,
where I find myself again. This is
the summer of my unfinished symphony,
a life cut back to the domestic bone,
chasing flies out of the kitchen,
the cerebral existence of a sparrow
eating grains, nuts, bits of green.
So farewell to the dancing. No more
getting drunk with the lost boys
telling the old tales: *how I lost my heart,*
how it broke, bled, how I gave it away
you say *easily*. All these years
it was only the proud pump in my chest
signing in moment by moment. Now
it has missed some of its step. Now when I say
I love with my whole heart what you get
is bruised, scarred, some part of it dead now.

* * * *

* * * * *

There were so many names, so many voices.
Now when I need it where is my voice,
for instance sitting in a train I try
counting my heart among so many beats,
and always my potential to drift off
into some other life and never come home.

Someone was here, where I am, the one
they call *the heavy breather, Sobersides.*
I have parts of his memory and think
he was more fun than I am, muttering
my way through the dark, frightening
the children. As for him he couldn't hear
what his heart said, too busy killing himself
and at the end with one last cigarette,
one last double and one last madman's dance
sang farewell the music. Telling his tale
a life he did not live he was never
at the event, at the feast with the candles.

Now wherever he is that I was, wrecked maybe
on some beach with the rest of the flyblown
plastic detritus, living under a rusty tub
with the name gone forever from its side,
when here I am answering his letters,
paying his bills, signing books he wrote,
picking up his pieces, sitting in his shed
all summer long, writing *Heart*
like the fennel root. Heart
like a great horseradish. Heart
like a loaf of hot bread new minted
from the oven, keep beating,
brave messenger, bearing news of yourself.

First echo

I recall the high trees rocking in the wind,
across the road where the soldiers drilled.
They learned their trades there, and went to war.
Beyond was unknown country, fields and distance
where the sun went out.
        One day my shout
among the tall trees found its echo there,
bouncing my name back among the elms,
calling and calling at the house back
and a second out of time the voice of *not-me*,
repeating all I said though what I said
was only *I, I, I am*...

How does anyone write anything?
How do they begin, in what gesture,
in what moment of a prayer, the pen
to the paper? What would anybody say?

Braille transcripts

1

Winter comes to the northern plains,
winds tearing the landscape, searing
the leaves then stripping them. Rust
is on the dust, an edge on the sedge
and the party is truly over. Find me
if you can in all this whiteness, in
the cries of birds flying south, the
patterns frost makes on the window's
glass. I'm here, somewhere. Find me.

2

The octet for strings, then applause
like the rain. 'Rain falls every day
here in our lives, with fog from the
river but rain chiefly on this rainy
coast': the barman telling his tales
I listening to what I shall call his
Reflection of a Tenpin Bowler: under
his foot the bone growth and new hip
are one with the pelvic swirl, stop,
foot stamped down and away that ball
went into a full deck, he made money
that way, again turning to the optic
and repeating *but the rain, the rain
on this accursed coast.* St Petersburg
that's where he'd rather be, *one day*
he says. Just switch on the TV, plug
in the phone and the air conditioning
and bet down the line. That's living
he says. Away from the endless rain.

3

Simple returns: we plant snow-drops,
tulip, crocus and daffodils, against
spring. Tom-next-door's dead and his
apples sour, and Johnny-two-doors-up
was beaten and robbed, in this quiet
neighbourhood. So where is that song
I sang once, moments a bird homed in
the sky and the river in its valley?
Where did that poetry go to, a shore
of only the waves' long arrivals? It
grows late and darker in the year, I
grow older eating a poor man's feast
of beans for my supper, reluctantly.

4

Indian summer. The road flecked with
gold, the plane trees full of birds,
their songs flooding the sunset. 'My
heart is dying' I say, testing it on
the air's autumn breath. I can't see
myself in these thickets, in so many
voices I've lost my voice. The back-
yard fills with wind, with the odour
of mints, rosemary, a shock of white
heads is the cornflower. In the last
of the foxgloves a last brown bee is still
fumbling his music. Day by day
it grows earlier late, the day's end
is blue, and gets closer and closer.

The furniture game

She's far away, beyond seas and the mountains.
Her easy presence makes her absence difficult,
not my heart more fond. She's the good wood
of which this furniture is made, she's everywhere,
in old sweaters, things made easy with wear,
leaving her shoes around. That drives me crazy.
In old fiddles sleep the sweetest tunes, they say.
Oh my love, my lily, my songs of the nightingales,
my sweet magnolia, come round the mountain.

Epitaph for a gardener

All his life a soldier in the field
at war with the weeds, the grass
rooting back faster than he tore it up.
At peace now it blows over him: *green, green.*

The annunciation

Many have laboured to convey it:
this moment that will trouble
centuries to come.

She was spinning, according to some,
working a tapestry, taking a walk
in the cloister, or as Da Vinci has it
reading a book.
          A dove or an angel
announces the news in a shaft of light
that is God's impregnating glance,
his most important announcement to date.

Here at any rate she looks properly
sceptical. Just as she might be
under such unexpected circumstance this is.

Venetian pieces

The Chamber of Torment

Outside men groan, caged in the square,
buried with their feet sticking up. In this room
the strappado has heard all their pleading,
the nailed planks have witnessed their replies.

It's all very simple: a plinth and a rope,
a long stem of agony hung from the roofbeam,
and the man drops, breaks, babbles whether he prays
hourly, at nightfall, or to the man in the moon.

Or whatever you wish, signors, I beg you
throw my brother in there behind the curtain,
take my friend Giovanni Giacomo who deserves it
for the money he's owed me these 15 centuries.

Casanova in the room of the Inquisitors

They take the blindfold off: wigs,
courthouse ritual, marble, polished wood.
Underfoot the black and white tiles
confuse the feet and trump the eye.

They will take you through the cupboard
to the rope, the hard boxes under the lead.
Does anyone here know you? Will anyone speak?
What is it you're accused of?

Love, I guess. Love brought me here
to confess all, answering *Yes* the dancer,
Yes the Armenian, *Yes* Edurne whose name
means *snow* and *Yes* the dark witch of Calabria.

But it's not what they want. They want
the names of my accomplices, my secret recipes,
who taught me to play so sweetly my instrument,
who taught me to whisper to make the clowns dance?

Sinistra

Packed arrows, bones in their boxes.
A horned wolf's head. Masks, silhouettes,
always the face behind the face another mask.
Egg white stones in the grass.
In the pine cone a tiny snake.
All over the honeycomb city of whispers
pale saints in wire halos, rotting
in their boxes, holy arms, holy legs.

Take the left hand, through shadow,
the stopped door of water, the campo
of the church of Our Lady of the Dead End,
the magazine stand a cabinet of darkness
all through siesta, the birds asleep,
the book closed, speech cut in stone.
The city dreams itself on the slow tides,
imagines water that can be walked on.

In my dream I met a girl who said *Venezia:*
it means the place to come to, a dream
for those who do not dream. I believed
there was a time we were each other's star,
lovers in the long water, waist deep
working the estuary among the kelp beds,
rocked in the sea swell, centuries ago,
another life I never lived and never woke from.

Then a long cry ran down the alleys,
a bleak signal through the salizadas
of the window-shouters, generations fighting
over the squares, their shouts riding on the wind
across the Fondamente Nuovo from Dead City,
leaflike, whispering all the tears, howls,
groans and all there ever was to pray for
through the miserable ages: *pray for us.*

Round and around the Ghetto Nuovo,
repeating *our memory is your only grave.*
From here were taken all the Jews of Venice,
from the furnace to the furnace.
This is a cursed place in a landscape
of leaning towers that one day fall,
where men rose from the dumb sea to speak
yet said not much. Only the seabirds.

Only a ship's horn, rousing the afternoon,
thrashing of ropes and metal as the sea
sucks its timbers. Boats slip
their moorings, move on the water's glance.
The gondolas are water snakes, funereal
bent Venetian pricks, at night the shadow
of a shadow, clef of coming music, harness
of the ghosts of horses that they are.

And then a bell tells half the fourth hour
of the afternoon, the day begins again,
– two men at chess, a radio bursting briefly
into dancing music, through an opened shutter
a hand and a jug water the geraniums,
somewhere a piano plays a practice piece,
offstage a woman yawns, a cage bird sings,
an English voice says *but these are wild birds.*

The baron regrets

The light here. Sometimes
it is domes and clouds, sometimes water,
the oar's fin through the ocean's drowse.

I have not painted. Where I look
is everywhere a study in perspective,
the eyes' delight in their deception.

All afternoon boatmen walk to the horizon,
moving on the edge of dancing,
their speech always on the lip of song.

What could I add to this: yesterday
at sunset a proud woman on a bridge
singing aloud not for money but for love.

The wine's cheap. The waiters
flash me their smiles and sleek black bums,
counting the cutlery all through siesta.

I eat late and am steady by midnight,
weaving my way among reflections
home to the same dream: the city

adrift on its rafts, the weeds
in the bright sea choking the air,
fish belly-up and the city drowning at last,

these posts low in the water, clinging
much as they clung together, refugees
on the sandbanks, building with reeds.

Long ago. I've kept up my notebooks.
Otherwise a whole summer wasted in Venice,
the tracks of light across the distance.

Neapolitan interiors

Views around the bay

Far off now a city of apartments, passages
of ducted light the days grow older in.
A city of *why not?* and all the hours
hung bell by bell around the towns,
but the shaky earth's cracked and the core
jets out hot here. Some have little –
a chair on the street, a pack of cigarettes
to sell. Scent of basil, resin,
smell of fish, bread, stink of traffic
always on the move along the bay's eye
losing sight in the blue haze of itself
between the mountain and the bay.
See this and die.
                    Out on the night water
two men fish the dark, one with a light,
one a spear. Inland Orion glints,
clearing the cliff, where the dim lamps
shine all night in the house of the dead:
Giovanni et Famiglia, Rosaria, Longobardo,
all their children folded in the drawers
stacked to the roofbeam, each a candle,
each a bell's intermittent random tongue
counting in the saints, the packed
municipalities squabbling along the coast.

Ercolano's message

Begins father forgive me, today I learned
but one word *oziosamente*, asleep in the sun
among the brown stones, all the guides
to the buried town nagging in three languages.
I have been between life and life, stone
by stone in the rich dust where the lizards
are at home – Papa Lizard, his inamorata,
his busy mates and their many bambinos.

Where was wineshop and water gossip, oven,
mark one man left on another man's wall
that he owed him, some inscription to a tart
she's a sweet fig, a vine, a fruity lotus.
Caught side by side in the sudden dust:
old or young with their offspring, a slave
grinding his bad teeth, Pliny the Uncle,
townsmen, dead all as all the dead are.

Buried. Stopped rooms in which to fight,
make love, spin, dream or wake suddenly
to cockcrow and children or the other birds,
the long shush of the night sea, finished.
No one here but an old man with his ruins
muttering in the kingdom of the lizards
spent prayers to the failed gods: *nothing's
sure nor long sacred. Message ends.*

A traveller's question

I have been days, years on the road,
sinking in winter, dreaming of the south.
I am who sets out who never arrives,
arrives though he never departed, the self
always talking to the self. I am one
changed by a journey whose tale's never true.
Therefore who is it crosses the littoral,
the wind faintly with rosemary, at night
glimpses in the cold bouillon of stars
himself? I have grown weary being part
of God's interminable education. Again
the dark sisters whisper in the walls,
and again through the rocks the wanderer
Odysseus mast-lashed and mad unstops
his ears to the singers on the wind,
all the songs on the radio telling him
nothing so well endures as the ruin of things,
a young woman lights up an old man's dark
but it won't last. Not much changes.
Whatever set the slow stars in the sky,
the Plough and the Pole to steer by
and all the blue jewels of the moon
doubled in the sea with the evening star,
more to the point will I ever get home?

Postscript: *nunc pro tunc*

Roman, I'd retire to the coast from things
public, – greed, power, the grim lusts
of the merely ambitious, all the sad wants
most men have merely to be remembered.

Devious or discontent, our doings
shabby deals in an alley, cutting throats
for loose change, thereafter soon enough
retching up again on the flophouse floor.

I would retire to Ercolano, where I'd be
resident cynic, the large events so far
beyond my notion or my wish. Slowly
to my own design I'd build a good house.

Between the mountain and the sea, my nets
slung under the olives, I'd fish a little,
sleep much, contemplate the grape, take
a long view of the town's doings and write.

The magic of Poland

One:

the coast a long ribbon of string,
green earth, woods. Then immigration,
not user-friendly.

Try to find a bar, and when you find one,
a beer. Try to understand the money
you got for your money. Stay warm.

Take a long tour of the monuments:
these are to all the many years the ravens ate,
the long depredations of the wolf, the bear,
the arrival of the Adam Smith Institute.

I write you, love, from Nova Huta,
from Kraków the soured beauty, another night
at the Palace of Culture I'll get weepily drunk
for you and for the magic of Poland. *Na Zdrowie.*

Two, the waitresses in Old Town

They are discussing shoes, footwear, feet,
limping and clucking like chickens
picking over their patch but too old
for the pot now. He wants her maybe
once a year at Christmas. By now
he'll be home asleep on the couch
or dead drunk on the floor. Her friend,
she had a pair of sandals, perfect,
but they stopped making them, closed
the factory. He doesn't love her any more.

Three, the music of the Emperor

Farms and unfenced fields,
villages, chained cattle,
turkeys, road signs
reading *Muzeum Oswiecim*:

Auschwitz-Birkenau.
Flat grey earth,
Pits, drains, factories.
The machineries of death.

Work will make you free,
Anna Sophia from Hamburg,
Jelena from Kraków,
tenants of the Ghetto Nuovo.

So close, far away as the moon,
as all the lives all the dead lived.

An offshoot of the rail,
tracks ending in grass, chimneys,
a tangle of old wire,
a pond of white human ash.

Four, the photograph

Time stops here.
And I am not in it. These chipped bowls,
piles of clipped hair, tangle of spectacles
are here for no one.

Beyond this moment nothing ever changes
but the yellow light across the fields,
bleached in the snapshot, fading out, the corner
of the picture turning inward where it burns:

a field of brick chimneys, the horizon
dirty smoke. Nothing beyond this:
a deathless landscape
with the heart burned out, the smile intact.

Monument

In which the bronze mouth forever opens,
a stone calling for stone, flags,
marches, bullets. *Freedom* he calls it
in the black metalled letters next his initials
chiselled into the bottom left hand corner.
The date. A handful of old flowers.

In which his raised arms are the hands
of the ventriloquist forever talking to himself,
the ego telling itself the same lie:
palm out in the signal to be still and listen,
the other a fist and a finger pointing
into the future, which completely ignores him.

Zoo Station midnight

Drunks glitter in their liquids, fish
far down water where the light dies
on their armour of metal plates and crutches.

Outside in the city flowers of smashed glass,
the faithful in black spider armbands are back,
and the firestorm raging these forty years.

The animals wander the trapped streets,
furiously wounded. Here comes the midnight train
from Friedrichstrasse, from Warsaw, from Moscow.

It arrives in a flurry of flags and snow
with wolves howling, taking the width of the night
to get here. It arrives dragging the sheets

of its landscapes, – peasants, fires, shoes, no shoes,
speeches, snags of barbed wire, bayonets,
the apple blossoms of spring, the marsh air.

Late again he says, the stranger at my elbow,
bastards, sucking on a beer. In his black coat
and white hair he may be my double, my dark brother.

He knows a bar, a taxicab, a place to stay,
a woman, it takes a little paper money,
a word from him and we'll be out of here and into history.

Katja's message:

'This sentence has no meaning,
but what are you going to do about the crocodiles?'

In Berlin, attempting sleep, this sentence
without meaning keeping me awake;
one by one the hours climb the clock,
labour as slowly down the other side.

The silence at the border is absolute,
full of watching darkness, wire and neon,
the dark trees either side without wind
or weather or the baying of dogs.

It goes on and on, the silence, a lake
without a name where legends surface:
a bead of air, a log of wood, a skin,
an eye blinked open in the dark.

It is the crocodile, easing down
into another sleepless night
along the border, here beside the wall,
where still this sentence has no meaning.

The Wall
(Obligatory)

There is the one side and the other,
and between there is the wall. Each side
has its monuments, its flags, its currency,
its bulletholes, its notions of the other.

Over here we say *the beaten in the lobby*
of the crestfallen. Some days we pity them.
Over there they watch us through binoculars.
Over there they call us fascists.

There, here is *over there*, and their maps
of where we are are coloured white,
as ours are of them. No one
over there can fall in love over here.

Here the street ends and there's wall,
and on the other side the same street:
tramtracks, kerbstones, streetlights
coming on, pedestrians about their business.

They do not wave or look back. It is
as if we were each others' ghosts. Either side
history comes with a wall round it.
We are each other's terra incognita.

Somewhere there's a piano playing boogie,
and on this side a late night argument
strung out with booze and bamboozle
till the word gets lost in the many

qualifications of itself, and it all ends
in tears. Over there the long silence
broken by dogs at each change of shift,
some border guard on his two-stroke.

And everywhere it seems a night bird
fills the dark with long pulses of his song.
He doesn't care to be one side or the other.
His song is all of him.

I understand where this late night music
of a sad piano is coming from.
I understand where that long
leashed baying of manhounds is coming from.

But I don't understand where the nightingale
in these long pulls of music through himself
and the buildings and the trees
or from which side of anywhere he is singing.

Passing through
(for John)

Travellers in a new country, arriving
without change for the phone, between trains,
just passing through. *You should have called*
distant friends say. *Ich verstehe Bahnhof* I reply.

Then we meet, drinking in another doomed city,
down streets named for dead soldiers,
victories understood only in the vernacular,
and we with our own debased currency another history

glimpsed in the driving mirror, central Europe
on fast forward: printout, flags, bullets,
disbelief on the faces of the tyrants,
end of system without escape clause. Walls fall and men.

As ever we're struck by odd presences –
six porcelain urinals in a row, their mouths open,
the white tiled wall, in the half open door
a brush waiting to be used, our faces in the glass.

There is a perfume called Sorrow.
There are bars, twilight, the sweet dark music of the city,
blossom, the faces of women, but is there time
to write the book of deeds before it's out of date?

Chinese whisper

I am a labourer on the Chinese Wall, one of thousands. Far from where I was born, I do not think of it. I was brought here with my neighbours, and set to building the wall. Our life is work, rice, sleep. All day from dawn to dusk I take my place in the line of men labouring up and down the mountains, heaving one by one the rough chiselled blocks of stone from the man on my left to the man at my right shoulder. I am indistinguishable from either one, my thoughts could be either of theirs. When one of them dies he is replaced, when I die the line will move up in my place, and the stones go on climbing the mountain, assembling into the wall. Only the wall grows, but we will never see it. Ahead of us, empty country; behind us the wall, perfect, new, cresting the ridges, enclosing the wastes, dividing the farmlands from the desert. We eat, work, work, eat, sleep, moving over the country with our many arms and legs like a long dragon. When at dark we sleep, exhausted, our sleep is the hard sleep of the same heavy stones moving up the mountain, down the other side. And memory. Asleep, still handling the stone blocks, I sometimes glimpse far away, impossible now, red willows by a river, a fish leaping, white lily flowers in the water.

After Brecht

In the end it is Joachim with his maps,
Thora in her garden: roses, lilies,
the scents she desires so she grows them.

It is the sunlight, high
through the tall evergreens, the birdsong,
the afternoon wind in this place, and our voices.

Telling our tales. We grew up on the other side
of a long long war we all lost.
Years have gone by. All our lives have.

With songs, sometimes music, children,
some love in this old cold world,
years of many letters and a few kisses.

It will always be so: this moment,
the sunlight, the long afternoon, the blackbirds,
Joachim with his maps, Thora in her garden.

Ken Smith was born in 1938 in Rudston, East Yorkshire, the son of an itinerant farm labourer. He has worked in Britain and in America as a teacher, freelance writer, barman, magazine editor, potato picker and BBC reader, and has held writing fellowships at Leeds University, Kingston Polytechnic, and Clark University and Holy Cross, Worcester, Massachusetts. From 1985 to 1987 he was GLA writer-in-residence at Wormwood Scrubs prison. He lives in East London.

Smith's first book, *The Pity*, was published by Jonathan Cape in 1967, and his second, *Work, distances/poems*, by Swallow Press, Chicago in 1972. Poems from these two collections and from a dozen other books and pamphlets published between 1964 and 1980 (including *Fox Running*) were brought together in his Bloodaxe Selected Poems, *The Poet Reclining* (1982; reissued 1989), which does not include work from *Burned Books* (1981) or his later Bloodaxe titles.

In 1986 his collection *Terra* was made a Poetry Book Society Recommendation and was also shortlisted for the Whitbread Prize. In 1987 Bloodaxe published his collected prose, *A Book of Chinese Whispers*, and a new collection, *Wormwood*, also a Poetry Book Society Recommendation. His latest book of poems, *The heart, the border* (Bloodaxe Books, 1990), is another Poetry Book Society Recommendation.

In 1989 Harrap published *Inside Time*, Ken Smith's book about imprisonment, about Wormwood Scrubs and the men he met there. This was published in paperback by Mandarin in 1990.

Ken Smith was working in Berlin when the Wall came down, writing a book about East and West Berlin: this turned into *Berlin: Coming in from the Cold*, published by Hamish Hamilton in 1990 and in paperback by Penguin in 1991.